Working with Cor

GW01080183

After 5000 copies of the first edition h
world an updated version of this popular book nas been prepared by
NCC's own careers staff, reflecting the current situation and working
trends in computing, especially in the areas of salaries and career
prospects.

The book now covers the following topics: 'What is a computer and
why has it become so important?' which introduces the reader to the
principal types of equipment that go to make up the computer system;
'Computers at work' outlines the history of computers and briefly
describes how modern computers work using examples from business
and industry; 'What computers do' describes the variety of different
jobs available to the newcomer and afterwards discusses the career
paths that may be pursued; 'Your computer education and training'
details the most common courses of entry and finally, 'Where to get
more information and training' which provides a useful list of publications and addresses.

Although the book has been prepared mainly for school leavers,
university students and other young people, it also offers guidance to
those who have already graduated, and others interested in the
possibility of finding a job in computing after experience in some other
field. Careers advisors have found it invaluable, and each year more
and more are turning to it as their main source of reference in this field.

Other titles of interest:

    Factfinder 12: Computer courses
    First-entry programmer
    Introducing computer programming

The National Computing Centre Limited is a non-profit organisation financed by industry, commerce and government. It is dedicated to promoting the wider and more effective use of computers through-out the economy. In realising its objectives the Centre

gives *information* and *advice*

provides *education* and *training*

promotes *standards* and *codes of practice*

co-operates with, and *co-ordinates* the work of other organisations concerned with computers and their use.

Any interested company, organisation, or individual can benefit from the work of the Centre by subscribing as a member. Throughout the country facilities are provided for members to participate in working parties, study groups and discussions and to influence NCC policy. A regular journal – 'NCC Interface' – keeps members informed of new developments and NCC activities. Special facilities are offered for courses, training material, publications and software packages

For further details get in touch with the Centre at Oxford Road, Manchester M1 7ED. Telephone: 061-228 6333

or at one of the following regional offices

Belfast	1st Floor 117 Lisburn Road BT9 7BP	Glasgow	Claremont House North Claremont Street C3
Telephone:	0232 665997	Telephone:	041-332 0117
Birmingham	Prudential Buildings St. Philip's Place Colmore Row B3 2PL	London	Audrey House Ely Place EC1
Telephone: 021-236 6283		Telephone:	01-242 1044
Bristol	Royal Exchange Building 6th Floor, 41 Corn Street BS1 1HG		
Telephone:	0272 27077		

Working with Computers

A guide to jobs and careers

PUBLISHED BY NCC PUBLICATIONS

Keywords for information retrieval (drawn
from the *NCC Thesaurus of Computing
Terms*): Career development, Conditions
of employment, Job hunting, Remuneration.

First edition published 1971

© 1975, THE NATIONAL COMPUTING CENTRE LIMITED

Published and printed in the United Kingdom of Great Britain and
Northern Ireland

ISBN 0 85012 126 4

Set in 10 on 11pt. Times through the NCC CAPRICORN computer-aided
publishing system and printed by Wright's (Sandbach) Ltd., Sandbach,
Cheshire.

Contents

Acknowledgements

The NCC staff who have been involved in the preparation of this book would like to thank several members and staff of the British Computer Society for their valuable advice and assistance. They also thank Miss Laura Tatham for her notable work as overall editor and contributing author to the first edition.

CHAPTER 1

Introduction

Our Purpose

This book has been prepared mainly for school leavers, university students and other young people. But it also offers guidance to those who have already graduated and others interested in the possibility of finding a job in computing after experience in some other field.

At present, many of those working with computers came into their jobs through experience with business, industry or some other field. This was natural and inevitable, for computing, as will be seen in Chapter 2, is no sudden phenomenon but has evolved from older methods of calculation and information handling.

This will change, at least to some extent. Computers are now well established, their use is constantly growing and the nature of the tasks for which they are used becomes more and more ambitious. This will lead to an increasing need for people who have had a systematic basic training in computing and therefore think naturally in computer terms.

Nevertheless, there are still – and probably will be for some time – areas where people who have acquired other skills can find useful, challenging and rewarding work. One of these is systems analysis and design, which cannot be carried out successfully without sound background experience and knowledge of business methods and practices but does not, as a rule, require profound technical knowledge of computers. Another is after-sales maintenance which can often, after additional training, be carried out by engineers qualified in related subjects such as telecommunications or have served in an appropriate branch of the armed forces. A third is in teaching – a field in which those well qualified to teach but hitherto lacking computer knowledge may often usefully serve after further training. In the manufacture of computers, too, retraining often successfully equips quite mature people without relevant experience to work in electronics.

To the young, computing offers some of the most challenging job opportunities available today. Most of these are as suitable for women as for men, and in some fields women excel. It is noteworthy that in this country and elsewhere women have done outstandingly well in the computer field. Chances for their successors are at least as good, for career prospects are seldom, if ever, affected by sex discrimination.

It is important to point out that many young people reading this book are likely to be thinking of a career in one of the many established professions. Computing plays an increasingly important part in many of these, and you will find that working for a qualification will allow you to take options in the application of computing to the profession in question.

Personal Qualities

Computing, however, is not a subject to play with. Qualifications are not gained overnight, as you will learn from this book. Persistence and hard work are necessary for success and there are other attributes and characteristics whose possession is important for real achievement.

First, perhaps, comes intelligence. Courses in computing science and other less comprehensive forms of education demand intelligence above the average, particularly ability to reason logically, and can never be considered as "soft options".

Patience and determination are necessary, too. Successful use of computers depends upon the application of rigorous logic and this, in turn, implies meticulous attention to detail. Every step must be carefully tested, every error identified and rectified. This is often a complex and time-consuming undertaking – there are no short cuts to success.

Then there is communication – between man and man and between man and machine. As we shall see, in *programming* the challenge is to use the machine as efficiently as possible by the precise and skilled use of special languages. In *systems analysis and design*, accurate and effective communication must take place between the specialist and the ultimate user – and this demands clarity as well as patience. It is equally important to establish satisfactory communication between one specialist and another within the computer field itself, for success in computer projects depends upon the collaboration of teams of such people.

Creativity is not, perhaps, a quality you would immediately associate with computing. Yet this is, in some senses, the most valuable attribute a computer person can have. While there is, on the one hand, a need for meticulous attention to detail, this is complemented by a need to think broadly and boldly. Progress in computing (as, indeed, in any other subject) is not achieved by timid adherence to old concepts but by innovation. This innovation may derive directly from man's approach to the machine (via programming) or from the invention of new ways to solve perennial problems (as occurs in systems design). Creativity is also, of course, of great significance in the area of research, design and development of computer machinery.

We would not want to suggest, though, that you must be a *superman* or *superwoman* to make an effective contribution in the computer field. Those who possess some or all of the qualities outlined above in quite modest measure are valued members of computer teams all over Britain and elsewhere. Just the same, we believe it important also to emphasise that computing offers tremendous opportunities for the outstandingly talented individual of either sex.

Perhaps we should also point out that it is not only the 'boffin' who finds rewarding work in computing. The introvert who gets completely wrapped up in his work to the exclusion of almost everything else can find his niche, but contributions of equal value may be made by more outgoing types who derive a good part of their job satisfaction through contact with other people. These points will become clearer as you read the book.

Layout of the Book

We have tried to achieve two objectives. Firstly, to give you the feel of what computing is all about; secondly, to present to you, in reasonably compact form, the practical information you need to embark upon a job or career in computing.

For this reason, the book is made up of a combination of text and tabulated information. In its earlier chapters we have tried to set the scene, show you how computing has evolved, how its application has grown and how fundamental a contribution the computer makes today to the quality of our everyday lives. Next we emphasise the over-riding importance of the human contribution. Then we outline more specifically what this contribution is. And finally, we show you how to start, where to get information – and where you may expect to move when you choose a career in computing.

CHAPTER 2

What is a Computer and why has it become so important?

Counting has always been tiresome and from very early times men have invented ways to make it easier. The first form of aid was the Semitic abacus which was in use in the Tigris-Euphrates valley in 3000 BC. It consisted of a tray of sand in which lines were drawn and pebbles were moved along the lines to represent numbers.

By the sixth century BC the Chinese had developed another kind of abacus – a rectangular wooden frame fitted with wires on which beads were threaded. Counting was done by moving the beads along the wires. So efficient is this method that right up to 1946 it was more used for calculation than any other device in the world – and was faster, too. Strange as it may seem, a rather similar principle is employed in modern computers. But here the 'beads' are thousands of electronic switches, which are fixed in position, and operations are performed by passing pulses of electric current through the switches.

The Renaissance

Blaise Pascal is credited with inventing, in 1642, the first machine that could perform the four fundamental operations of arithmetic – add, subtract, multiply and divide – and he did this to help his father, who was a customs official. In 1671, Leibnitz improved on Pascal's original design by making a machine that multiplied and divided directly rather than doing this by successive additions and subtractions as the earlier machine had. But although astronomers, physicists and mathematicians needed to do a great many calculations, the machines were too unreliable to come into widespread use.

11

Charles Babbage

It was not until the nineteenth century, when precision engineering became possible, that satisfactory mechanical calculators could be manufactured. Production of cash registers and desk calculators first began about the middle 1800s.

Meantime, Charles Babbage, a British mathematician, had conceived the idea of a machine that would carry out a sequence of operations and print the results automatically. He was encouraged to do this by the discovery that many of the mathematical and scientific tables in use contained errors, often the result of careless typesetting and proof reading. So in 1812 he designed a machine he called the Difference Engine that could compute and print mathematical tables.

Later, Babbage planned another machine – the Analytical Engine – which would carry out operations in sequences determined by patterns of holes punched into cards fed into the machine. This plan was unfortunately too ambitious for the technical capability of the time and after Babbage's death in 1871 his ideas were forgotten. It was not until 1939 that work began in the United States on the machine based on a similar principle – the Automatic Sequence Controlled Calculator.

The Age of Electronics

Fast growth in the volume of routine calculations of all kinds produced a need for equipment that would operate faster than any machine, containing moving parts. In consequence, scientists both in Britain and the USA began to experiment with electronics.

The speed of a mechanical device is limited by the fact that metal parts must move. In electronic devices, though, there are no moving parts and an electrical impulse can move at enormous speeds. Numbers can be represented by passing a tiny electric current through devices such as thermionic valves, which can be switched on and off. If you have a row of valves, all of which are switched either on or off, you can call the 'on' state 1, the 'off' state 0, and you may represent any number by a combination of ones and zeros. This is similar in principle to morse code in which numbers are represented by dots and dashes. This method, in fact, is used in computers today, though valves have been replaced by transistors and even smaller circuit components.

In 1946, a device that used electronic principles was produced. ENIAC (Electronic Numerical Integrator and Computer) differed from computers in use today in one very important principle: control of the sequence of operations was effected through switches set by hand. This meant, of course, that some of the benefits gained by electronic speed were cancelled out. The next step, therefore, was to store operating instructions within the calculator in the same way that numbers were stored – an idea first proposed by an American, J von Neumann, in 1946. The first stored program computer began operating at Manchester University in June 1948, and the first machine to be used in commerce began work in J Lyons & Co. in 1953. (Incidentally, in computer circles the word 'program', which you will often encounter in this book, is always spelled in the American way.)

All today's computers operate on stored programs of instructions and it is this characteristic that makes the electronic digital computer different from all other calculating aids. The word *digital* is used to describe all the computers talked about in this book which are the kind of computers that operate with numbers (and letters of the alphabet represented as numbers).

Another type of machine, the *analogue* (or analog) computer, calculates on a different basis. It is far less generally used, and much less versatile, for the kind of work covered in this book, and is therefore not described here.

How the Digital Computer Works

Though computers are complex, and are made up of many very ingenious electronic devices, the way they operate is really quite simple. In a way, it is misleading to talk about 'a' computer because a computer is in fact a whole group of machines linked together. Each of these machines has a different use, as we shall now see.

The heart of the computer is the *central processor*. This contains the arithmetic unit in which the calculations are done, and the internal storage or memory unit (whose job is much the same as that of human memory). It also co-ordinates the work of the whole group of machines or devices.

Information from the outside world (that is, from the user) reaches the central processor through an *input* device. There are many different kinds of unit that do this job and the description 'input' is therefore a general one. After the computer has carried out its calculations or other work, it must return the results to the user. This it does through an *output* unit – also a general term that covers several different types of device.

In the computer world, the word *data* is used to describe all types of information fed to the computer. Information going to the computer is therefore called *input data*, while results coming out of it are called *output data*.

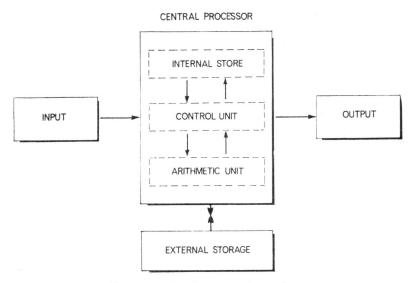

Components of a computer system

You will notice that data moves between the internal storage unit and the arithmetic unit. Data held in the store can be worked on in the arithmetic unit and results then returned to the storage unit. This method is, in fact, very like the one you use when you 'save up' a figure in your memory as you carry out calculations in your head.

Like a human being, the computer has only a fairly small memory so for much of the information it must use during its work it relies on 'files'. These files, known as external storage units, are described later.

The unit of data is known as a *character* and may consist of a digit, a letter or a symbol; examples are 3, p and * respectively. Characters may be grouped in numbers or 'words'.

INTERNAL STORAGE

The memory of the computer usually contains two types of information: the list of instructions on how it is to carry out the task it is doing at present – known as the *program*; and the information it is using, the data. When, for example, the computer is told to determine the length of time the motors of a rocket should be turned on to make a course correction, it must have a program that tells it how to do the calculation and data which describes the present position and course of the rocket.

EXTERNAL STORAGE

In ordinary life, almost everybody whether he is a businessman, an engineer or a scientist working in a laboratory, keeps a great deal of background information in files. So a computer is also provided with files which the program tells it to look up when necessary.

When the computer is instructed by a businessman to make a ledger entry on a bank account, it needs a program, data about the amount of the cheque and other details and *file* information about the present state of the account of the person who wrote the cheque.

WHAT THE COMPUTER CAN DO

Though computers are used in thousands of different ways, they can perform only very few different kinds of operation. They can, of course, add, subtract, multiply and divide. They can take in data, store it in memory or in files, and can move it from place to place. They can also recognise certain conditions – eg whether a figure is plus or minus or one amount is larger or smaller than another. But this is all.

Why, then, is a computer considered so powerful and important? First, it is the ability to do these things at high speed. A fast modern computer can add two and a half million 19-digit numbers together in one second! This speed enables it to cope with large amounts of work in a very short time. So it allows us to do calculations that could never be carried out by people with pencil and paper or even by other kinds of machines. And it is a feature of our life today that more and more of the things we do require the handling of very large amounts of information.

Secondly, it is human ingenuity that enables a man to describe very complicated tasks in a way that allows the computer to handle them. In practice, any task that can be described and handled by a known method can be programmed for a computer.

The Equipment

You and I communicate with one another by speaking and writing. But as yet, though much money is being spent on research, it has not been possible to design machines of reasonable cost that can recognise speech or freely written handwriting. This is partly because there are so many differences in things like accent and the shapes of hand-written letters. At present, therefore, if we are to communicate with computers we have largely to use methods that convert information to a form that can be accepted by the machines we have at present. All the characters of data we wish to input can quite easily be changed into various kinds of code to suit machines. This is the same kind of conversion you use if you change letters or numbers into Morse or Braille, though the machine codes are different from these.

INPUT METHODS

One of the commonest ways of changing input data into codes is through *punched cards*. The blank card is like a postcard and the characters are recorded by punching holes on a machine that has a keyboard rather like that of a typewriter. Usually there are 80 columns on the card and in each column 12 punching positions. A character is denoted by perforating two or more holes in a column, so that on one card it is possible to record 80 characters.

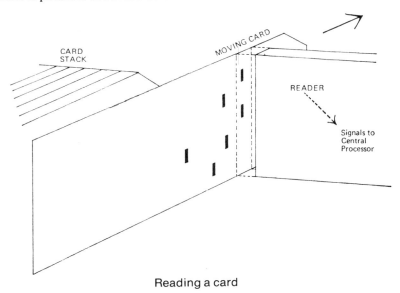

Reading a card

A similar principle is used in preparing data on *paper tape*, but instead of a card a long paper ribbon is used, and a row of punching across the tape represents each character in a coded form.

Information punched into tape or cards is placed in a special input machine where the paper passes under an electronic 'eye'. The beam from the eye shines through the holes on to a very sensitive device that converts the pattern into tiny signals that are acceptable to the computer. At present, characters on cards can be read into the computer at speeds of up to 1000 characters per second; with paper tape, speeds are up to 2000 characters per second.

Another way of recording data is on *magnetic tape* of a kind very like that used in a home tape recorder. Here, the operator again uses a typewriter-like keyboard but the characters, instead of being punched, are recorded as magnetic signals. The tape is read into the computer by another kind of input machine whose reading speed is much faster than that for punched cards or paper tape.

Another way of presenting input data to the computer is through *optical character recognition* (OCR). This sounds like a contradiction as we have already stated that computers cannot read in the way we can. In fact, however, there are now machines that can read characters imprinted by other machines with a very distinctive type, or digits only when very carefully written by hand. Others can interpret as characters small marks handwritten at certain pre-determined positions on forms. At present, however, application of these machines is still somewhat limited since dirt or other accidental marks on the paper or poorly formed characters may prevent accurate recognition by the reader. OCR input can, however, be read at up to 2000 characters a second. This would be equivalent to handling, for example, gas bill 'stubs' for 70,000 consumers in an hour.

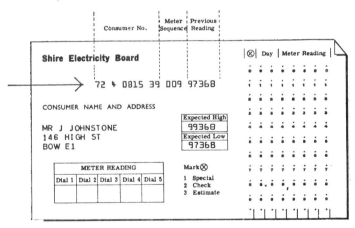

Optical characters

Magnetic ink character recognition (MICR) will be familiar to most cheque-book owners as the rather oddly-shaped characters at the foot of cheques are designed to be read by this method. The characters are imprinted by a special typewriter-like machine whose ribbon is impregnated with an ink-containing substance that can be magnetised and thus read in an input machine. This method overcomes the danger of inaccuracy due to dirt and marks. MICR characters can be read at speeds equivalent to handling over 60,000 cheques per hour. Readers are often built into larger machines which sort cheques mechanically into pigeonholes after they have been read electronically.

STORAGE DEVICES

All the devices described in this section exploit the property of magnetism. The importance of this is that all forms of magnetic storage are re-usable (like the tape in your home recorder) in that the act of recording (or writing, as it is called) destroys the signal that was previously there.

INTERNAL STORAGE (MEMORY)

The form of storage device most commonly used today is made up of thousands of tiny doughnut-shaped metal cores placed at the junctions of an intricate network of wires. For this reason, the memory is often referred to as *core store*. Each core holds the information '0' or '1' and several cores are needed to store the code for a character. Core stores are made in a way that enables the computer to pick up the information from them very fast; but as they are expensive to manufacture they are used only for main memory where high speed is of the utmost importance.

EXTERNAL STORAGE (FILES)

The devices used by the computer for maintaining file records are sometimes called *backing storage* units instead of external storage. Data is recorded on various forms of magnetic media which are put into handling devices attached to the central processor. The magnetic media can often be exchanged in the handler so the user can have a 'library' of such files.

Magnetic tape is much used for computer files, in addition to its use for recording primary input data. Magnetic tape provides a relatively cheap form of bulk storage. The processor may have several magnetic tape handlers attached to it onto which any tapes from the 'library' may be loaded for processing.

Data can be either 'read from' or 'written to' a magnetic tape by the central processor at speeds up to 100,000 characters per second or more. The drawback with this medium is that information on the reel can only be reached 'serially'. That is, if you want to deal with a particular customer's account record it may take some minutes to reach it, since a computer reel holding perhaps 20 million characters can take 15 minutes or so to process. This is a very long time – in computer terms.

The limitations of this serial method used by magnetic tape have been overcome by other devices. There are, for example, *magnetic discs* which are rather like gramophone records and are plated with a special substance. Two types are in use. Large (20 – 40 inches in diameter)

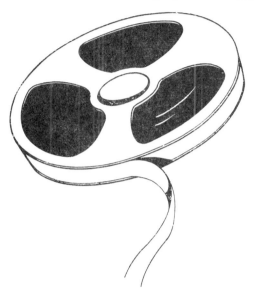

Magnetic tape reel

fixed discs that are permanently linked to the computer and exchangeable *disc packs.* The latter consist of a number of discs stacked one above the other which can be loaded onto the handler spindle when needed. One read/write head is provided for each surface.

Discs provide what is called *direct* access. This means the computer can jump straight to the particular piece of information it wants – in no more than one-tenth of a second or so – without running through irrelevant matter first.

Direct access is also provided by *magnetic drums.* These are large cylinders which revolve at very high speed and are coated with a special substance. Read-write heads are fixed along the edge of the drum where they reach information recorded on tracks on the periphery of the drum. Drums are normally permanently fixed to the computer and cannot be exchanged with one another as some discs can.

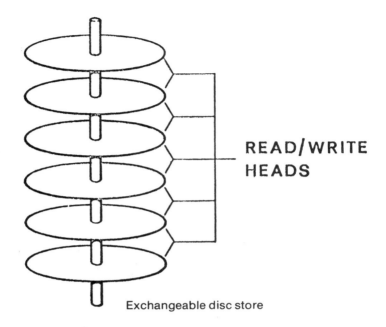

READ/WRITE
HEADS

Exchangeable disc store

Both discs and drums can store enormous amounts of information. Typically, their capacities are of the order of 50 million characters.

CONTROL AND ARITHMETIC

It is the job of the control unit to co-ordinate the actions of all the various parts of the computer. Both it and the arithmetic unit consist of thousands of electronic circuits. Use of new techniques has resulted in great reduction in the size of modern arithmetic and control units compared with that of early computers.

OUTPUT EQUIPMENT

As the computer finishes its calculations or other work, it must return the results to the user. Information, to this point available only in the form of tiny electrical signals, must be channelled to an output device that will translate these into a form that can be accepted by man.

By far the most popular output device in use at present is the *line printer*, so called because it prints an entire line at a time. Printers like this use great lengths of continuous forms or plain paper (with or without carbon paper and additional sheets) on which they imprint as many as 24,000 characters a second – 1500 or more lines a minute. Since the paper may be up to 18 inches wide, this means that the entire contents of an average-length novel can be printed, line by line, in under three minutes!

Sometimes results produced by the computer may be needed for further work by the same or another computer at a later date. In this case, output may take place (instead of, or as well as, on the printer) on cards or tapes which the computer itself punches. Results may also, of course, be written into magnetic files for future use.

Some information has more meaning for the user if it is presented in the form of a picture of some kind, such as a graph or a drawing. The computer can, in fact, be made to produce pictures like this through an output device called a *digital plotter*. This device is fitted with a pen which can move from side to side across a fixed bar while the paper unrolls in a direction at right angles to this. By programming the computer to control the movements of the pen, maps and diagrams, etc, can be made.

Another twenty minutes output . . . . .

INPUT/OUTPUT DEVICES

In addition to machines used solely for input or output there are devices that perform both functions. These enable man and computer to communicate more directly.

The simplest of these devices is a *typewriter*. All present-day computers are equipped with a typewriter at the operator's desk, and on this the computer (controlled by the program, of course) prints out information on what it is doing and the operator, through the same machine, gives additional instructions to the computer. Typically, the computer might report that it had finished one of several programs it was working on at the same time or that its printer had run out of paper. The operator might tell it to give priority to one of several programs which until then had all been treated as equal.

Typewriters are also used extensively today as *remote terminals*. This is the general term used to describe input or output or input/output machines located at places far from the central processor. Data is sent to and from the computer through an ordinary telephone line. In this case, the user at the far end uses his keyboard to contact the computer and input his data; and the computer prints out the finished results a few minutes – or possibly even seconds – later.

Another input/output device that is growing in popularity is a machine that looks like a TV screen with a typewriter keyboard in front of this. This is called a *visual display unit* and is also used as a remote terminal. Here, as the user types the words they appear in light on the screen; and the computer shows its results in the same way. You may have seen clerks in travel offices use devices like this to find out if a seat is available on a plane you want to travel in. Many airlines have hundreds of these terminals some of which are situated literally thousands of miles from their computers.

TV-type screens of the type mentioned so far can show only letters and numerals. There is, however, a more elaborate (and expensive) kind that can also display pictures as complex as those that may be drawn on a plotter. The user himself may also actually draw in light on the surface of the tube using a device known as a *light-pen* and the drawing is recognised by the computer which receives it as data. This equipment is particularly useful to design engineers who may make an initial design in this way and instruct the computer to analyse it for, say, strength and rigidity. If the design is unsatisfactory, the designer makes some modification by altering his drawing on the screen and the computer re-analyses. This process continues until a satisfactory design is produced. This computer method is far faster and more efficient than the old paper-and-pencil method.

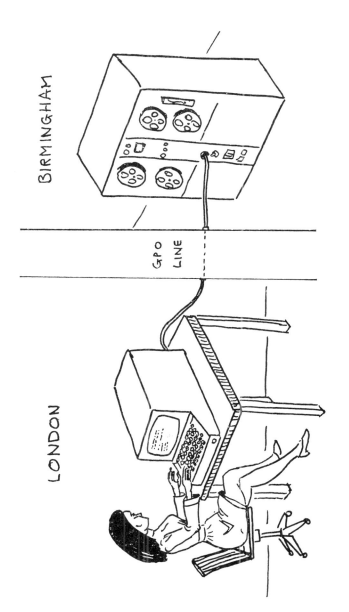

Remote visual display unit

Variety is the Spice of Life

The great variety of equipment for putting data into, and taking data out of, computers exists not because none of it is wholly acceptable, but simply because people want to do things in so many different ways. With these riches at their disposal, it is not surprising that new applications for computers are being uncovered almost every week.

But the advance is really not fast enough. The trouble lies, not with the lack of capability in the computers themselves but, in the scarcity of people trained in the skills of using them. This is a very important point to remember and one that was mentioned earlier: the only way in which a computer can be of any use is through the people who write its instructions and devise the systems on which these instructions are based. No computer ever made can take action on its own. Without man, a computer is nothing but a collection of extremely expensive – but entirely useless – equipment.

At one time the power of computers was used only in solving technical problems. Their ability to do arithmetic at the speed of light was directed at the mass of calculations involved in solving such problems as occur in the fields of nuclear engineering or radio astronomy.

One of the characteristics of scientific work in general is that the amount of calculation is very large compared with the volume of input and output data. In some problems, for example, one might feed the computer with a single equation and name the beginning and end of a whole range of data to which you wished this equation to be applied. This could involve the computer in a vast amount of calculation whose result (the one thing you asked for) might be printed out as a single line. In projects like the Moon Landings, huge volumes of calculation had to be performed by computers on relatively small input and the results applied to quite a few instruments.

Business problems, on the other hand, often involve very little calculation but large amounts of sorting and printing. For example, a typical Electricity Board sends out 25,000 bills a day. The arithmetic simply involves subtracting the present meter reading from the previous meter reading and multiplying the result by the price per kilowatt of electricity, at the same time making allowance for the various rates at which customers are charged.

Early computers, therefore, did not make much provision for fast input and output, but those of today are designed to accommodate the needs of businessmen as much as those of the scientist, or engineer.

In the next chapter we look at some of the many ways in which computers are being used in the world today.

CHAPTER 3

Computers at work

In Chapter 2 we introduced you to the principal types of equipment that go to make up the group of devices called a computer. We outlined the various ways in which information is translated into a form which the computer will accept and the ways in which the computer produces answers intelligible to the human beings who use it. Finally, we emphasised that the work computers do is the result of the ways people have invented to use the machines and that without this human contribution the computer is useless.

Computer people use the term *hardware* to describe their equipment and to distinguish the machines themselves from the programs referred to as *software*. It might seem to you unnecessary to make this differentiation; but in practice it is not always easy to distinguish between the two. The ways in which modern computers work are extremely complex and when something goes wrong it may not always be easy to discover whether the fault has occurred in the electronic equipment or in the detailed programs that tell the computer how to deal with its work. Another, rather facetious term sometimes used is *liveware* to cover the people involved in running the computer and preparing systems for it.

The Earlier Days

But to return to our hardware:the variety of input and output devices have had considerable influence on the ways in which computers have been used. Thirty years or so, before computers came on the scene, punched cards were used to record information that was later processed in electro-mechanical machines which, for instance, sorted the cards and printed out the detail recorded on them. It is natural that, when computers came along, the same kind of punched cards were used.

Naturally enough, too, early users of computers tended to follow patterns already established in their organisations. Many companies that had punched cards to provide, say, information on customers' purchases, went on to use the computer to provide not only bills for goods and reminder notices about unpaid bills, but also to analyse under various headings what goods they had sold, to whom these were sold, the success of the salesmen and so forth. In theory, it was possible to get this information by using mechanical sorters, but in practice it took so long that the information would have been too out of date to be of any practical value to the company.

Similarly, research workers, who for many years had used electro-mechanical calculation machines, originally employed computers as nothing more than extremely fast and accurate calculators. To them the computer's ability to do arithmetic was more important than the means of input and output. This was because the scale and complexity of calculations was often very great, although the amount of data needed to start the calculation and the amount of information needed at its conclusion was very small.

As the computer industry grew, these two early areas of development – handling accounting routines and calculating complicated sums – moved steadily closer together. For instance, it was quite easy, while sending out bills to customers, to collect very detailed information on exactly what things customers were buying. And it was found that when this past history was subjected to a series of mathematical calculations, it was possible to predict with some accuracy how the company's customer demand would shape up in the future. This was a big step forward from merely calculating and printing up bills.

By the late 1950s, one of the most important features of computers was recognised: this is that the central processor can be programmed to carry out a wide variety of tasks. Other machines are generally built for a particular purpose; but computers are general purpose, that is, the same machine can be used for fast scientific calculations and for large-scale business work. This is not to say that every computer is ideally suited to every kind of task. It does, however, mean that the user may largely determine the range of work it can do through his choice of storage media and of input and output equipment.

The Range of Use Today

It will give you some idea of the range of jobs that computers are doing if we take a typical day and see what part computers play in it.

If you manage to get up early enough to enjoy breakfast, you may begin with a cereal. Its manufacturers have used a computer to analyse the answers to questions they have put to hundreds of people who eat cereals for breakfast. As a result, they have chosen a recipe that ensures its flavour and texture are just as you like them.

The egg you eat next was laid by a hen whose life history – eg how many eggs she laid, at what times, whether they were of good quality – was kept with that of thousands of other hens on a computer file. Breeders use this information and make all kinds of complex computer calculations which tell them which cocks and hens mated together will be likely to result in chickens that produce the best eggs.

Your journey to school or work may take you along part of a motorway. The chances are that the amount of concrete and other materials that went into it, its cost and the amounts of ground that had to be cut away in some places, the size of valleys to be filled in in others, were all calculated by computer. And, when the road was being planned, the computer may well have been used to calculate the cost of, say, by-passing a town instead of going through it. In a few areas in this country, traffic lights are controlled by a computer. Special machines count the cars that go past various points, and pass this information to a computer programmed to change the lights to red or green under certain conditions.

If your destination is school, then the timetable may have been planned by – well, you know what! Though the timetable may seem quite · simple to you, it is in fact a complicated job to see that everybody gets the correct number of hours' teaching in every subject he studies and that the teachers are neither under- nor over-worked. In some schools, experiments are in progress to find whether computers can help to teach children by printing out questions and using answers given by the pupil to determine which question to ask him next.

Meanwhile, at home the postman has called and there is a letter telling you about a new gardening book. This letter has gone to thousands of people whose addresses are kept on a computer file and the computer has printed the labels for the envelopes. If there is a bill from the gas or electricity board, this will certainly have been prepared by computer. Soon computers will be used to sort letters – and that is why we are now asked to use post codes.

When the housewife goes to the supermarket she will find everything she wants. The supermarket owner has used a computer to keep records of what is sold each day and produce a list of what each shop needs to keep its shelves full. The delivery vans that bring these goods visit a large number of branches each day because the computer has worked out the quickest route to travel between the various points.

A call at the Post Office to collect the family allowances involves another computer in keeping a tally of the payment. If money is drawn from the giro or a bank, the computer will be informed and will subtract the sum involved from the balance on the account.

More Examples, still, as the Day goes by

At lunchtime, a news broadcast says that a much-needed kidney has been flown from Europe to a patient in a British hospital. When this kidney was offered, a computer compared the details of the kidney with those of every patient awaiting a transplant and selected the one most likely to benefit. The passenger plane that flew the gift to this country was designed with the help of a computer, a computer was used to reserve seats for the passengers and computers helped to guide the pilot and assure his safe landing.

After the kidney was rushed to the hospital and the patient operated upon, a computer may help look after him. Sensitive instruments attached to his body will be linked to a computer using a program that compares the detail received from the patient with information held in its files. In this way, it assesses when any harmful change occurs in the patient and issues a warning signal to the nurse in charge. Before long, some British hospitals will keep patient's records on computer files. So if a man has been brought in unconscious from the street and someone knows his name, the computer may be asked to display on a TV-type terminal details of his medical history – including such important details as his blood group.

Across from your home, a new block of flats is going up. A computer estimated its total cost, helped the builders to get the various stages completed on time by warning them when work was falling behind, and calculated for the architect how thick the walls and girders must be to make the building safe.

Some at least of the type that appears in your evening paper was set by computer. And it is likely that a computer in the factory where the paper on which it was printed was made, kept watch over the manufacturing process to ensure even thickness right through the sheet. Perhaps you will watch commercial TV this evening. A computer may well have reserved the time each advertiser wanted and arranged the order so that two pet food ads did not appear one after the other.

And so it goes on. If you look around you will find many examples of how computers quietly contribute to the pattern of our daily lives. It is remarkable how one machine has so permeated nearly every aspect of public and private life in less than 20 years.

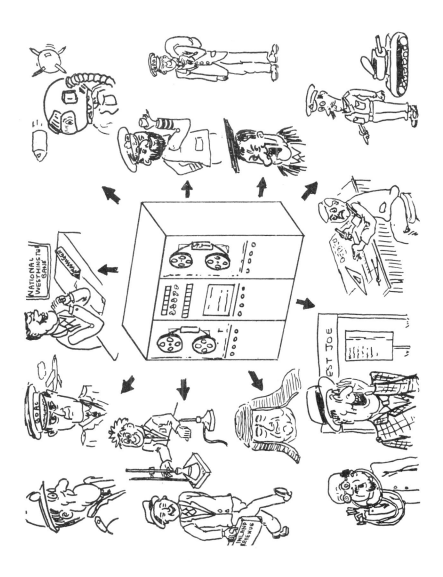

The Computer in Business

Turning from this broad picture, let us look in more detail at the work a computer does for a single company that we will suppose is in the engineering industry – one of Britain's biggest and most important activities. We will look at the history of computer development in this company which has had a computer for five years.

It is likely our company's first computer was used to handle the day-to-day accounting – calculating wages, preparing invoices and monthly statements, recording incoming payments and printing reports on the flow of money and the pattern of expenditure and income right through the business. Used like this, the computer would provide such information more quickly and accurately than older methods could; but it would not make any major contribution towards running our company more efficiently.

In a manufacturing company, the two most important aspects are marketing (selling) and production (the manufacturing processes). So we should look more closely at these to see how the computer could help.

New Products

What products does the customer want, in what quantities and when? If marketing is to be efficient, these questions must be answered. So the company sends out people to question customers or studies its own products to try to find out whether all are satisfactory and whether it could usefully make any additional ones.

If the data collected during this research is recorded on standard forms these may be handed to girls to convert into punched cards or some other input medium. The computer will then produce lists which show what customers like, what price they are prepared to pay, what they expect from the product and so on.

After studying these reports, the marketing manager decides to prepare a specification for a new product. This is passed to the Design Department who, like most people faced with this kind of job, find there are many routine calculations to be made. They might have to analyse the stresses to which the product will be subjected in use so as to make sure that all parts will be strong enough. If the product includes a motor, they must calculate how powerful it must be and how big. Much work of this type is repetitive and it is possible to write standard computer programs that can be used every time such calculations are needed. To test his new design, the engineer describes its characteristics, what it is supposed to do and what it cannot do. This detail is fed to the computer which analyses it automatically.

The design agreed, the Engineering Department decides how it is to be made. By this time, though, the company has set up a computer file listing all the tools and parts the company uses. So it is simple to list all the requirements for the new product and get the computer to separate these into lists; things the company already has in stock; things it must make itself; and things it must buy elsewhere.

Into Production

The new product will be only one of a number the company is making. So the next task for the production manager is to draw up a manufacturing plan.

Production planning is very complicated. Its starting-point is a forecast from marketing that predicts what products (including the new one) customers are likely to buy during the next few months. As each product is made up of a lot of separate parts, this requirement must be broken down, or 'exploded', into lists of totals of all parts needed.

If he is to do a parts explosion, the production manager must have a record of exactly what parts go into each product. Some parts will be used on more than one kind of product (for example, if the factory makes several models of typewriter, each will need a set of keys). So a total must be made of how many of each part is needed to complete all the products to be manufactured – and when these are needed.

Some of these parts will be brought ready-made from other manufacturers. But many will be made in our factory on a variety of machines by men with different skills. Then more men will be needed to put these and the ''brought-out'' parts together. So the production manager must know how many, and what kinds of, men and machines are available. And because both are expensive, he will want to see, if he can, that all are kept fully employed during working hours and that as little overtime as possible is done. All the time, though, he must remember that the marketing forecast predicts there will be demands for the goods at certain times.

Without a computer, the production manager and his staff may take weeks to draw up a production plan. And in the end, they may find the plan won't work. Perhaps it means leaving some of our machines idle for part of the time and putting work out at others. So he has to revise the plan — more weeks of work. But if he keeps all the information used in the planning on computer files, the computer will, if necessary, produce several alternative plans within a few hours. And if, later, the plan must be revised because an important machine broke down, the computer will do this too, provided it has been given information on how much work has been done so far.

Getting the Materials

Once the production plan has been adopted, raw materials and parts must be ordered from outside suppliers. This is the responsibility of the Purchasing Department. Unfortunately, so much work is often involved in placing the orders and chasing suppliers who have failed to deliver that the buyer has no time to do his proper job – looking for new suppliers who might fulfil the company's needs more economically.

This would not happen if the company made up a computer file that lists all its suppliers, and another on which stock records are kept. When, on looking over this file, it found that fresh stocks were needed, it could automatically print an order for the appropriate supplier. And, if the goods do not arrive (their arrival would have been notified by the Goods Inwards Department and details fed into the computer) it will prepare a reminder notice to the supplier in question.

The stock file would contain a list of all the parts used to make the company's products; it would also record how many of each part is available in stock to satisfy production needs. By analysing past usage, it would tell the stock controller when it was time to place a new order and this request would go to the Purchasing Department.

Satisfying the Customer

As customers' orders are received for the goods the company manufactures, details are given to the computer. The computer looks at its finished goods stock file and sees that what the customer wants is available. It therefore prepares a bill for the customer and a note to the Despatch Department who will then send off the goods. At the same time, it will subtract the number of items sold to the customer from the finished stock record and make a note on that customer's ledger account (held on another file) of the amount of money owing.

If the product had not been in stock, the computer would print an acknowledgement telling the customer when the goods will be ready (information it gets by scanning the production plan held in its files). Meanwhile, it has been building up a list of orders received, and if it finds the totals differ greatly from the expected number (as provided by the sales forecast) it will print a report for the management who will then decide whether it is necessary to revise the production plan.

Each week, the factory foremen note exactly how much has been made and this detail goes into the computer. The computer then, by comparing this with the production plan, can produce lists of what jobs are to be done by what machines the following week.

Other Work for the Computer

This account by no means lists all the ways in which the computer could be used by our engineering factory. One more very important job it could do, for instance, would be to keep track of all the costs incurred during manufacture and compare these with estimated costs. The reports it produced would enable the management to see exactly how the company's money was being spent, and if they found this unacceptable, to decide what must be changed. Even the things described here are fairly routine jobs for a computer today. Many companies have even more ambitious plans in hand for using a computer to help run their business.

The Way Ahead

As we mentioned in Chapter 2, it is no longer necessary to have the computer near at hand to be able to use it, since distant terminals – and even smaller computers — may be linked to it through telephone lines. Information stored in a computer is available very quickly. This means that for a company with several factories, only one computer might be needed. One large central computer could prepare a plan for all the factories and could notify a manager who badly needed a certain part whether this could be obtained from one of the others in the group. Or there might be a large central file of information on stock availability for a whole industry so that when one needed a particular item one could simply dial an "Engineering Supplies" computer to find out where the nearest stock could be found. No file of this kind yet exists, and the technical ability and other considerations needed to construct it would be great. Just the same, it is already quite within the bounds of possibility.

A Universal Tool

In this chapter so far we have tried to give you some idea of the kinds of ways in which computers are being used today. We have, however, concentrated rather strongly on commerce and industry, and this may have led you to suppose that undertakings like this are the principal users.

This is by no means the case. The power, speed and ability of the computer to handle very large quantities of information and calculate with extreme accuracy is also put to good use by all kinds of professions. A lawyer, for instance, who must often cite a previous case to back up his argument, could get a computer to pick out one he wants instead of searching for hours through books.

Engineers who build bridges and dams, aircraft – and computers – depend heavily upon computer-processed calculations. Many of the power stations that supply our electricity are partly or wholly controlled by computers. The huge lightweight domes that form roofs for buildings like a modern sports stadium could never have been designed without a computer to do thousands of sums.

Economists whose job it is to observe and predict the trends in every aspect of the movement of money and other resources obtain more accurate results than could ever be hoped for in earlier days by feeding the data and complex mathematical programs into their computers. Town planners use their computers to determine features varying from the requirement for pubs to the width of roads and the most satisfactory size of drainpipes to lay. No designer of an airport or docks today would fail to employ a computer to help him find a layout that would satisfactorily accommodate the predicted volume of traffic.

In the USA and in Switzerland, children are saved from death by poisoning because a computer, supplied by the doctor with data on their symptoms, searches its files to find what they have probably swallowed and names the remedy. Slowly, the world's art treasures are being catalogued on computer files. Computer calculations helped architects safely to shore up York Minster when it was in danger of collapse.

The list is, literally, endless, for new applications and better versions of old ones are being discovered every week. What is needed urgently – now and for a long time to come – is people with the ability and imagination to allow the new possibilities to be realised.

How Big is the Scale?

There were probably as many as 8000 computers installed and working in the United Kingdom by the end of 1974, and this number will grow considerably in the following years. Very many more people will begin to use terminals for remote access to a computer, and the numbers of such people – and their terminals – will increase at a higher rate than the actual number of computers itself.

Outside the United Kingdom, the USA is top of the "league table" with an estimated 100,000 machines now in use. Western European countries are in some cases ahead of the United Kingdom in relation to size of economy, and it is particularly important that this country becomes and stays in the forefront of computer usage, when economic union is a strong possibility.

More machines means more skilled people to handle them, and Chapter 4 gives an idea of just how many will be needed within the next few years.

What Computer People do

So far, we have outlined the history of computers, have briefly described how modern computers work and have chosen a few from thousands of examples available to illustrate how computers are used to good effect in almost every walk of life.

We have emphasised how only the human contribution allows us to make use of computers. The time has now come to discuss this contribution in more detail.

This chapter is intended to provide some detail of the jobs associated directly with the use of computers and will, we hope, be useful for quick reference. In subsequent chapters you may read what kind of people will employ you, what is the full range of work available in the computer field, what educational and professional qualifications you should acquire and what career prospects you may expect (including the current salary range).

Nearly all the jobs to be described lead to more senior posts, in which the work of more junior staff is supervised, and there are good opportunities to move on to management positions. The question of career prospects is covered fully in Chapter 5.

There are various sequences in which we could have listed the jobs. We might, for example, have put them in order of importance as determined by salary scale. But to do this might involve false comparisons of the kind which prompt people to ask: who is more valuable to society, the dustman or the symphony writer?

So, neatly dodging this awkward issue, we have placed the jobs in an order related as closely as is practicable to the computer processing function itself. As such, we must begin with Systems Analysis and Design.

Systems Analysis and Design

In Chapter 2 we stated that any problem that can be specified, and to which there is a known solution, can be passed to a computer. But sometimes the hardest thing is to specify the problem, especially when it relates to the complicated procedures used in business and industry, some of which were outlined in Chapter 3.

Another complication arises from the fact that a computer, though immensly fast and accurate, can fairly be considered as stupid. So unless one describes to it in minute detail and with perfect logic what one wants it to do, it will either get hopelessly "stuck" or produce answers that are quite absurd. It is only, perhaps, when one uses a computer that one fully appreciates the value of plain human common-sense!

The instructions the computer itself will use are prepared by a programmer whose job we describe later. But the programmer's skill lies mainly in his ability to exploit the computing machinery; and because he is often not too knowledgeable about how the user can best apply a computer, he generally relies on someone to state the basic problem for him. This statement is prepared by the systems analysts and designers and is used by the programmer in much the same way as an engineer uses a working drawing.

In business, particularly, a computer is seldom used to make the first attack on the problem. Generally, up to the time the computer was introduced, people have tackled their work by other methods.

So the job to be done by the systems people falls into two broad parts: firstly, to discover exactly what is being done at present and how it relates to the needs of the undertaking (systems analysis); and secondly to map out a new system for use with a computer (systems design). Though the new system may embody many of the features of the old method if this was basically a good one, it should generally also contain much that is new. If this is not so, one may suspect that the power of the computer will not be exploited as fruitfully as it might. The same holds good if the user is exchanging his present computer for a more powerful one.

A "Job Specification"

Here, then, is a summary of the work that systems analysts and designers are expected to do:

1. *Participate in feasibility studies. These are made to find out whether or not a computer would be of value in the organisation thinking of using one. At this point, it is also very important to*

find out exactly what the prospective computer user hopes to achieve. (Strange though it may seem, this is often far from clear at the outset.)

2. Find out, precisely and in detail, what is being done within the organisation at present to achieve these objectives. If, for example, the computer is to be used chiefly for accounting, one must ascertain what accounting systems are being used at present.

3. Assuming that the use of a computer seems feasible, the systems men (and/or women) must prepare a plan of computer-based procedures that will handle all the relevant data and produce the required information. Frequently, it may be necessary to consider more than one way of tackling the problem and to select one as the most satisfactory, giving reasons.

4. Prepare a full report. This is addressed to managers, users, auditors and others whose responsibility it will be to authorise use of a computer. A good report will give detailed breakdowns of costs incurred in the present and proposed methods and include an estimated value for the new features provided by use of a computer. It will often, too, compare and contrast the abilities of two or more alternative computers that might be used, giving reasons for recommending one of these.

5. Write a detailed specification of the approved system in a form suitable for use by programmers. This will include the preparation of diagrams known as systems flowcharts.

6. Specify the volume and frequency of activity – computer and non-computer (eg how many invoices will be processed each month; the average number of lines in each) – as a basis of timing and costing.

7. Prepare appropriate working manuals for use by all those affected by the new system.

8. Assemble and prepare materials that can be used for testing the computer-based procedures.

9. Control the new systems or assist in getting them underway.

10. Check that the overall system meets the required objectives.

11. Review the system in the light of experience or changes in circumstances or objectives. (As life never stands still, changes in even the best computer-based systems are generally fairly frequent.)

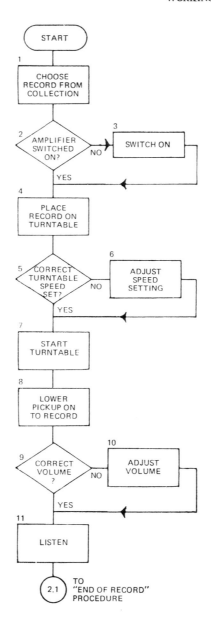

System flowchart —"Playing a record"

From this account, you will realise that systems analysts and designers are closely involved with the computer project, not only long before it takes shape but after the first programs begin to run smoothly. You will also notice that systems work is concerned at least as much with the human beings involved in the computer scheme as with the workings of the computer itself.

Programming

The programmer, with the computer's ultimate users on the one hand and the machine itself on the other, is the go-between. In other words, his job is to write a series of instructions that will cause the computer accurately and efficiently to put the user's intentions into effect.

A computer can work only when its instructions are strictly logical. So if the programmer leaves any loose ends, it will fail to operate satisfactorily and to produce the required results. There are, however, always many ways in which the desired results may be achieved. Much of the skill of the programmer lies in selecting the neatest of these, that is, in using the computer's resources to best advantage.

Programs are always written in special 'languages' acceptable to the computer. Many languages used today (known as *high-level languages*) quite closely resemble ordinary English or employ terms similar to those used by mathematicians or scientists in the course of their daily work. These languages are easy to learn and easy for programmers other than the original writer to interpret. Sometimes, though, it is necessary to use more complex and detailed languages whose purpose is, in effect, to allow the programmer to express finer shades of meaning in computer terms. These other languages, known as *assembler codes*, are harder to learn and test the user's skill more than high-level languages. A different assembler code is used for each make of computer (and sometimes for individual models within each manufacturer's range), whereas high-level languages may be used on any make of computer of suitable size.

Two Types of Program

Most computer programs fall into one of two broad classes. *applications programs* are designed to achieve one specific purpose – for example, prepare a payroll, keep stock records or analyse sales. *Systems programs* are intended to enable the computer to accept, organise and control the handling of the applications programs, a number of which may be processed simultaneously. Their object is to allow the computer to be used as effectively and economically as possible.

The need for systems programming, which is generally a good deal more complex than applications programming, has arisen only fairly recently with the development of computers that are far more powerful and versatile than earlier models. Today, some systems programs are provided ready-made by manufacturers since their absence would prevent most users from fully exploiting the capability of their computers.

Summary of the Tasks

Here is a brief list of the programmer's principal duties:

1. *Prepare detailed programming flowcharts from the system specification. These flowcharts show the basis of program design and are used for reference, during the writing and when changes are subsequently made.*

2. *Check the logic of flowcharts.*

3. *Write a logical series of applications or systems instructions.*

4. *Write and desk-check programs, written in appropriate languages.*

5. *Test the programs on the computer and remove faults so that the programs will give no trouble during use.*

6. *Write instructions for the computer operators who will run the programs. These instructions include routines to guide the operators in locating faults.*

Today, though small applications programs may be written by a single individual, most programs are prepared by large or small teams of people whose work requires varying degrees of skill. Their efforts are directed by a chief programmer (under whom there may be section leaders if the project is very large) who assumes ultimate responsibility for the design and operation of the completed program.

Data Preparation and Control

Data preparation involves, as we have already seen, the use of equipment to translate information from the form in which it is used by human beings into a form acceptable by a computer input device. In practice, this generally entails acquiring skills similar to those required for ordinary typing, plus special knowledge such as an ability to read by eye the codes punched into cards or paper tape, use of the punch machine's control keys, and so on.

As it is of the utmost importance that only error-free data reaches the computer, all information is verified. Verification generally involves duplication of the data preparation work by another operator who uses a similar keyboard but does not re-punch except when she detects a mistake in the original. Verification, though not completely fool-proof, succeeds as a rule in eliminating all but a very tiny percentage of error.

In a typical data preparation department all the operators are girls who work together in one room containing upwards of four machines. Their work is presided over by a supervisor whose skills in human relationships must be at least as great as those on the technical side of the job. The supervisor may also be responsible for controlling the flow of work through the department. That is, he or she ensures that all incoming work is registered, is made up into batches, is punched and verified to meet the day's commitments on the computer and is passed out to the computer room at appropriate intervals. In large data preparation departments there may be several section supervisors while the control task is handed to a separate person.

Computer Operations

Computer operations work is equally suitable for men or women. The task of these people is to actually run the machine by using the appropriate buttons and switches and by loading on supplies such as paper, magnetic tapes or discs and so on, and by taking any appropriate action demanded by the program and signalled by a message on the typewriter at the computer's control console. It is desirable for operators to have some programming knowledge. A busy computer installation may be manned in two or three working shifts, each of which is headed by a chief operator who accepts overall responsibility.

A Range of Duties

Summarised briefly, the duties of the computer operator are to:

1. *Set up the equipment and put it through any necessary running tests.*

2. *Assemble input data files and computer programs in accordance with a predetermined timetable or in response to priority demands.*

3. *Supervise the running of the computer during these programs and load up with supplies as necessary.*

4. *Monitor printed output and assemble this for delivery to the user.*

5. *Provide an initial diagnosis of faults in equipment, programs or other media (eg incomplete input data).*

6. *Maintain records of machine utilisation (a function sometimes performed by the computer itself).*

7. *Maintain conventional files and stores where program cards, spare magnetic tapes or discs, stationery, etc are kept. (In large installations, tape and disc files may be looked after by a 'librarian').*

Customer Engineers

The engineer is a person of key importance in every computer installation; and if this is of any size, an engineer may remain permanently resident. This is not because computers are inherently unreliable – in fact, their record in this respect would make the average car user green with envy! But they are delicate and the smallest fault may cause havoc with results. In consequence, a computer is put through certain routine tests at least once every 24 hours. Many organisations depend very heavily upon their computers and these may be fully loaded, so faults must be identified and rectified without delay.

Diagnosis

The sheer complexity of the electronics within a computer may make diagnosis of faults very difficult; and, as mentioned earlier, it may also be hard to detect whether error has arisen from hardware or from software failure. The maintenance engineer is provided with a variety of special instruments and with a number of routines that he may apply to diagnose at least some of the faults most likely to occur. It seems generally agreed, however, that the best engineers are those who develop a faculty akin to intuition which suggests to them what the cause of a fault may be. In addition to electronic maintenance there is, of course, a fair content of mechanical work since all input/output equipment contains mechanical parts for the handling of paper, etc.

Men with experience in telecommunication engineering or other fields closely akin to computers may sometimes be successfully trained to apply their skills in the computer field.

What are the Country's Needs?

Table 1 will give an idea of the growth in demand for computer staff in the United Kingdom. The figures show very clearly that a large number of people, and mainly young people at that, must be encouraged to join the exciting and challenging computer profession.

Table 1

Estimated numbers employed in the UK

	1972	1974	1979
Systems Analysts	21 000	29 000	45 000
Programmers	29 000	40 000	60 000
Operators	20 000	29 000	45 000
Data Preparation	54 000	57 000	70 000

CHAPTER 5

Your First Job – and Afterwards

As Chapter 4 has shown you, there are a number of different types of jobs in the computer world and each demands a different combination of skills, qualifications and experience. As we have said, there are also various levels of seniority, so that in systems work, for example, you will find junior, senior and chief analysts and in programming a similar kind of grading.

In this chapter we shall discuss the kinds of job open to newcomers, the career paths that may be pursued and the types of employer who offer positions. As this book is intended mainly for young people on the threshold of a career, much of the information relates to these. But those thinking of entering the computer industry after some experience in other fields will also find guidance on the kinds of opening that may be available.

Let us start first with the kinds of employer. They divide conveniently into four groups: computer users; equipment suppliers; computer consultants; and others. The first of these is by far the largest so we will take this first.

Working with Computer Users

Computer users are found in all sectors of industry and commerce as Chapter 3 will have suggested. It is not only business organisations who are seeking new staff; there is a demand also from Government Departments, Local Authorities, Electricity and Gas Boards, Nationalised Industries and many others.

Mainly, users' needs are for operators, programmers and systems analysts. For the latter category, some employers are prepared to take university leavers but it is rare for school leavers to be considered. There are, however, plenty of trainee openings in the other two jobs, so we will begin by considering the opportunities for operators.

Operators

In this section, we use the term 'operator' rather more broadly than in Chapter 4. So here you will meet not only computer operators but operators of data preparation equipment, and also two other types of operator not yet mentioned: those who use ancillary machines that are generally situated outside the computer room, whose purpose is mainly to sort punch cards and tabulate information; and those who use remote terminals of various kinds.

Data Preparation

In a user organisation, like any other, the first step in computer processing is data preparation. Sets of documents are made up into batches and passed to operators who punch the detail into cards or paper tape or magnetic tape in the ways outlined in Chapter 2.

The typical data preparation machine operator is a female, often a school leaver. If she joined the organisation without previous experience she would receive the basic training either from her employer or by attending a special course run by some outside organisation – perhaps a training specialist or the supplier of the equipment she will use.

For this job she will need a good general education since she may have to decipher poorly written documents and relate these to cards or other computer input she is preparing. An aptitude for and interest in figure work is an advantage as much computer input is in this form. Some 'O' levels, or the Certificate of Secondary Education would also be desirable though not essential. Some employers also like to be assured that the prospective operator is neat-fingered, so that the fact that she can type or even play the piano may count in her favour.

Selection is usually by personal interview and the girl may be asked to take some sort of aptitude test that will indicate whether or not she is likely to make a successful operator.

An experienced keypunch operator would have the opportunity to move into machine operating or to senior punch operator or supervisor given the right human qualities. It is only fair to say, though, that as a rule opportunities for promotion from keypunching are limited.

A small but growing number of organisations use magnetic tape encoders in addition to or instead of paper tape or card punches. Usually machines like this are operated by specially trained and previously experienced keypunch operators. Though the job is very similar to that of punching cards or paper tape, the equipment itself is more expensive and elaborate than that used for tapes or cards. As a result, operators are usually more senior girls and consequently higher paid. Their promotion prospects, however, are the same as those for keypunch operators.

Ancillary Machines

When information is punched into cards, users may want to sort these into some special order and list some of the information on them before they go to the computer. This sorting, controlling, checking and listing is done by machines – which need operators. Machine operators are generally trained on the whole range of user's equipment so they might well have had previous experience as punch operators. At first they learn to operate and control their equipment under supervision, having had specific training either by the equipment manufacturer or their employers.

Some girls find machine operating more interesting than data preparation because they like the variety of tasks. There are also, on the whole, rather better opportunities for promotion than generally occur in data preparation.

Computer Operation

Our data is now ready for the computer, so it goes to the computer room where it becomes the responsibility of the computer operators, whose tasks were outlined in Chapter 4.

What sort of person makes a good computer operator? An aptitude for practical work and a certain degree of manual dexterity are desirable as is that intangible but real quality 'a feeling for machinery'. The ability to think logically and clearly is also important, as is the capacity to keep cool when things do not go according to plan.

Prospective computer operators may be asked to pass an aptitude test and some employers expect them to take a programming aptitude test as well. It is also usual to expect them to have up to five 'O' levels, which probably include English and elementary mathematics.

Inevitably, a computer operator will spend a good deal of time on his or her feet, so suitable stamina is necessary. Very short or exceptionally

A certain degree of manual dexterity . . . . .

tall people may find the height of the machinery unsuitable and thus might get too tired. Almost all computer rooms are air-conditioned so the operators, though sometimes tired, at least never get hot as well! Shift working at unusual hours may well be required in some installations.

Training usually begins with a full time introductory course run by the employer or by the supplier of the computer. During this course, the trainee will learn something about computers in general and much more about the particular kind of computer he or she will operate. Approved courses are also available at various colleges, and these are covered in Chapter 6. Such a course can lead to the RSA Computer Operator's Certificate.

Prospects for computer operators are good. They may move on to be programmers, provided they have a satisfactory general educational background and the right kind of aptitude. More usually, perhaps, an operator can expect promotion to senior operator, or to shift supervisor if the installation runs more than eight hours a day. Before he can reach this position, however, he will have to broaden his technical knowledge and show himself capable of managing other people.

As many girls and women become computer operators as men, and there is no sex discrimination in either pay or promotion.

Tape Librarian

Many computer installations employ a person whose role it is to maintain and control the many magnetic tape and disc files used in the various applications. The security of these files is important and the job is an important one. It requires the same level of staffing as for computer operations and may appeal to a girl who has handled ancillary equipment.

Remote Terminals

The user who employs you may well have a central computer that in addition to handling work originated at the head office may do work on data produced at distant branches. This data may be sent by post or van; or it may be transmitted electronically through telephone or telegraph lines through remote terminals situated in the branch offices – as we saw in Chapter 2.

Many terminals have keyboards similar to those found on ordinary typewriters or on the various kinds of accounting machine now in use. Their operators, therefore, will have the same kind of training and career prospects as are available to keypunch operators. On the other hand, the terminal may not be in constant use, so its operator might be asked to do this job as only part of several duties she performs in the office.

Programming

Many computer users now offer opportunities for school leavers to train as programmers. What programmers actually do was outlined in Chapter 4, but what kind of person is best able to do this rather exacting job?

The programmer must be able to concentrate closely on small detail yet not lose sight of the final aim of the program. As a rule, he or she must be capable of applying original thought to a problem as well as being prepared to do the routine – and sometimes boring – work needed to produce neat and accurate program documentation. A programmer, you will recall, is responsible for testing out his work and ensuring it does the job it is intended to do. This may bring him into day-to-day contact with the computer and so it can be useful, though not always essential, to have at least some operating skill.

It is not easy to define exactly what qualities go towards making a good programmer. Certainly it is important to be able to reason logically and to have the patience to take meticulous care with detail. It is also necessary to be able to impose the self-discipline needed to work to the standards laid down for program design. The personal qualities of candidates should therefore reflect these requirements.

In a small user installation, an individual programmer may be solely responsible for writing a program. More often, however, each programmer is given part of a job, the whole being completed by a team. Here, then, the ability to work co-operatively with others is essential.

Trainee programmers, that is people without previous experience, may enter the field as school leavers at 18 years old. Several 'O' levels may occasionally be acceptable, though any degree of upwards progress is unlikely without further study. Prospects of promotion are better when the entrant comes in with at least one 'A' level. A useful alternative qualification is an Ordinary National Diploma or Certificate in Business Studies. Some computer users also have special data processing training schemes for graduates and these courses usually include a sizeable content of programming.

Other large computer users have developed programmer training schemes that take both 'A' level school leavers and university leavers.

One construction firm has developed a scheme under which school leavers are 'articled' to the company in rather the same way as a trainee accountant is articled to a firm or an apprentice is indentured. This means the trainee is committed to the company for two years during which he or she receives a very comprehensive business training in addition to learning programming skills.

Prospective programmers are almost always expected to pass an aptitude test and many may also be asked to take some sort of general intelligence test as well though it is as well to point out that many so-called programming aptitude tests are simply general intelligence tests. Final selection is by interview.

In a fair number of user installations, particularly those whose computer tasks will be fairly straightforward, efforts will be made to recruit programmers from among existing employees. Typically, the company invites anyone who is interested to take a programming aptitude test. Though this test is probably one of the standard types, some users do not impose the time limit allowed for completion that standard usage demands. By making this concession, they are able to include in the programming team individuals who, though not perhaps as well qualified as would be necessary in a large installation, make a useful contribution. A good deal of unsuspected ability has been uncovered in this way, successful applicants being by no means confined to those doing clerical or middle management work, or to those in their twenties.

Basic programming training (and training in relevant languages) will generally be achieved by attendance on approved courses available at various colleges (*see* Chapter 6), or on courses arranged by the supplier of the equipment the programmer will use. Some private study will also often be needed, and most employers allow time for this. The newly-trained programmer will, however, find that real expertise is developed only by practice under the supervision of someone more experienced.

Prospects for promotion, through junior to senior and finally chief programmer, are generally very good for people with real ability. Since the higher the job the bigger, as a rule, the number of people to be controlled and supervised, managerial ability is also generally needed.

How exciting a programming job is depends in some measure on how elaborate the computer system is, but even more on the type of application required by the user. Lack of funds or some other reason may induce a user to perform tasks on his computer that theoretically can be done only on a more powerful machine. This demands considerable ingenuity from the programmer. In addition, an increasing number of large companies today are launching very ambitious computer-based schemes whose main objectives are to provide the managers with any information they want, practically on demand. To program systems like this demands a high degree of creative ability in the programmer and thus offers an exciting challenge to those who have the right kind of mentality and are prepared to work hard.

The larger computer departments have a need for systems programmers of the type distinguished from applications programming in Chapter 4. The increasing use of elaborate general programs, made available from the equipment supplier and other sources, requires the detailed knowledge of specialists in this area.

Many programmers, however, hope to progress to systems analysis and design work. This quite often happens, though the fact that someone is a good programmer does not necessarily mean that he will make a good systems analyst.

Systems Analysis and Design

A systems analyst, as you learned in Chapter 4, must reduce the sometimes ill-defined systems used in business into some logical form, while the systems designer has to take a fresh look at these with the object of devising new systems for use on the computer. Both these aspects of systems work may, of course, be handled by the same person.

To be able to do systems work satisfactorily one must have a general knowledge of business and a more specific knowledge of the business of one's particular employer. It is also necessary to appreciate, at least broadly, how computers work, though depth of knowledge is not always considered necessary.

In these circumstances, and bearing in mind that systems work generally involves considerable direct contact with various members of the user organisation, you will not be surprised to learn that very few organisations will recruit school leavers for these jobs. It is, however, becoming more common for university graduates to be accepted and then put through a specially designed training course in systems analysis and design. On the whole, though, people are not very useful in this area until they have acquired the right kind of background experience in business and this does not generally happen until they have reached at least their mid-twenties. Training courses are available from a number of colleges as well as from equipment suppliers, as you will learn from Chapter 6.

These days, most people come into systems work from one of three directions. There are programmers – who generally need some training in business practices and principles; people already in business, who need training in computing; thirdly, university graduates who have undertaken – or must be given – extensive training on both the computing and the business aspects of the job.

Systems analysts and designers require imagination, creativeness, precision and the ability to work methodically. It is also most important that they should be able to form cordial human relationships, for their work often requires extraction of information from people not too willing – initially at any rate – to provide this, and the introduction of methods that may be resented chiefly on account of their novelty. This opposition is as likely to come from all ranks of management as from the ordinary office or factory workers. Only patience, tact and gentle persistence can change these attitudes.

It is almost impossible to exaggerate the importance of sound systems work to the success of a computer project, however modest or however large. This is understandable when you recollect that it is the systems people who form the link between the users of the computer and the programmers. Sloppy systems work will raise continual problems for the programmer. Unimaginative systems work will ultimately mean that the computer is not utilised as effectively as it might be.

A good systems designer may often find that the senior managers for whom and with whom he is working have less clear ideas than he of how the computer may be used to their advantage. When this happens, he must somehow induce these managers to formulate their long-term objectives and convince them how the computer can help them realise these in addition to aiding them to perform their routine daily tasks.

Success in systems work depends, then, on the ability to form successful human relationships as well as on technical knowledge, scrupulous attention to detail and the capacity to exercise creative imagination. At present – and probably for many years ahead – there is a desperate shortage of individuals who possess this combination of qualifications, and promotional prospects are therefore very good for the right kind of person.

Education and Training

An increasing number of users are running their own comprehensive schemes for staff development, and there are beginning to be a number of good opportunities for people interested in communicating ideas to

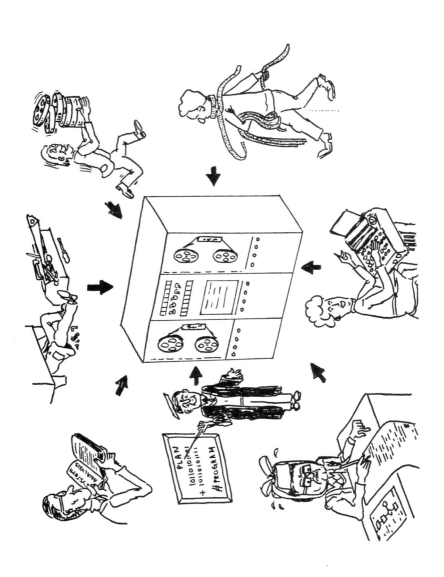

others. Appreciation courses for managers may well form part of the job and candidates for this type of work are likely already to have a background of systems work, and ideally some programming experience as well. A formal background in education is, of course useful but computer experience is the primary need.

Management Posts

In operating, programming and systems work there is plenty of scope to rise to management positions. Many people heading these activities in typical installations today are under 30 years of age, though some more mature managers – certainly in systems – come from responsible jobs elsewhere in the organisation.

The next step is to the job of Data Processing Manager, and a very responsible one it is too. Again, some DP Managers are recruited from among people who already have good experience of general management outside the computer field, but a considerable proportion of them have come up through the ranks of more junior DP staff. The manager at this level has overall control of all computer activities and may well report to a Director in some commercial organisations.

In Summary

Table 2 shows the normal career expectation with a computer user, and indicates *minimum* ages at which the various level of job can be attained.

Employment with Equipment Suppliers

Professional Computer Staff

Computer manufacturers, in addition to using computers to run their own business, undertake to help customers set their computers successfully into action. The manufacturers therefore employ the various kinds of operator, the programmers and systems people we have already discussed earlier in this chapter.

Qualifications are much the same as demanded by users, though manufacturers may well demand higher standards than are required by the majority of users.

At present, all manufacturers provide their customers with at least some basic software free of charge; and other software, including 'package' applications programs designed for use by a variety of organisations, are offered either free or for a charge.

In effect, basic software consists of a group of highly specialised programs. These are stored permanently by the computer and their purpose is to allow it to perform in as versatile and efficient a way as possible, whatever applications the user may put on it.

Work on software at this level is the province of the systems programmer, and demands a high degree of expertise and creativity. The word 'creativity' should not, however, be taken to imply that manufacturers

Table 2

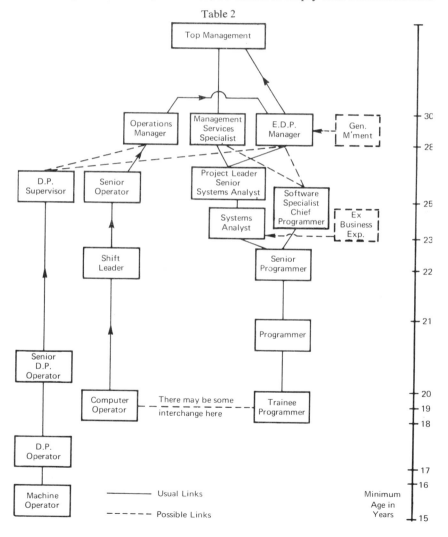

seek the wayward genius type. The kind of programmer most suited for software writing must, though highly creative, also be prepared to submit to the intellectual discipline of driving single-mindedly towards a stated objective and acting as a member of a team. 'Something of the atributes of a scientist, a bank clerk and a creative artist' is how one manufacturer summed up the qualifications required by those working on systems software development.

Equipment Design, Development and Manufacture

People of both sexes are required by computer manufacturers for research, design and development. Jobs in this area are generally particularly interesting because computer technology changes so rapidly. This is true not only in the electronics area. Equipment like card readers and printers, which embody a high proportion of electro-mechanical components, also change rapidly in response to unceasing demand for higher speed, more reliable performance, and so on. Optical techniques, for example, are applied in the reading equipment whose function is outlined in Chapter 2.

Most manufacturers run good apprenticeship schemes which accept boys and girls who wish to apply physics, mathematics, engineering and other disciplines to computer problems in research and development. Some firms offer two-year postgraduate apprenticeships to university leavers who wish to spend this period moving between departments to learn the business before choosing any particular job.

Manufacturers also recruit engineers, physicists, mathematicians and computer scientists straight from university and polytechnics to fill specific jobs.

Studentships are available on a 'thick sandwich' basis. These, open to candidates with appropriate 'A' level qualifications, involve one year with the manufacturer followed by three at university and a final year back with the manufacturer. As described in Chapter 6, degree courses at polytechnics are also applicable and then are often on the basis of the second year out of four in industry. At the end of this five-year scheme, most students are eligible for membership of their professional institution.

Polytechnics and technical colleges also offer 'thin sandwich' courses. These entail alternating periods within the firms and at technical colleges. Such courses are suitable for those wishing to read for technological degrees or higher national diploma. There are also craft and technical apprenticeships available which lead to ordinary national certificates and diplomas.

Undergraduate students and technician apprentices may either remain in research, design or development work or transfer to production or customer engineering.

Computer production departments require mechanical, electro-mechanical and electronic engineers as well as production engineers. Though many of these are recruited fully trained and experienced, some come through apprenticeship schemes of the kind already outlined.

It is also worth mentioning that computer manufacturers are glad to undertake the training of suitable men and women for production work which, again, tends to be more interesting than most because of fast-changing technology. The chief requirements are manual dexterity, concentration and, in some jobs, good eyesight because of the very detailed and delicate nature of the work. Entrants may come from very varied backgrounds and trainees of up to 50 years of age, or occasionally older, may be acceptable.

Customer Engineering

Manufacturers offer many openings which, as mentioned in Chapter 4, involve meeting customers, servicing and repairing their computers and sorting out all kinds of technical problems. People who wish to enter this kind of work (which also presents constant challenge due to changing technology and the growing complexity of the machines) should normally have an Ordinary National Certificate in mechanical, electronic or electro-mechanical engineering or the City & Guilds Telecommunications Certificate. In this connection, it should be mentioned that telecommunications expertise is of growing relevance in the computer field, owing to the fast increasing use of remote terminals and other forms of data transmission network.

People who have served in one of the technical branches of the armed forces are often welcomed into after-sales maintenance jobs.

School leavers are also required as apprentices, or may enter after-sales maintenance after completing apprenticeships in other engineering branches.

Marketing

'Marketing' is the word used in business to cover all the activities directly and indirectly associated with the selling of a manufacturer's products. Those who come under the supervision of the marketing manager will therefore include sales promotion staff, people responsible for arrangement of conferences and exhibitions, the advertising department and public relations personnel as well as sales managers and salesmen.

Computer manufacturers have openings from time to time for people in all these activities. Since, however, the relevant qualifications relate more to expertise in some aspect of marketing than technical knowledge of computing, discussion of these posts is outside the scope of this book.

The one important exception is computer salesmen and sales managers and it is the duties of these we shall discuss now.

Selling Computers

Computer salesmen are very different from the salesmen who sell articles such as groceries or lawn mowers, for in addition to the ability to sell successfully they require considerable technical knowledge of computing and of the ways in which business, industry and other computer-using activities are run.

Most computer manufacturers recruit their salesmen from graduates of any faculty and also take some people with appropriate 'A' level passes – though this is less usual. All those recruited to work in marketing are trained by the manufacturer in all aspects of the job. Because the activities of computer users today are so varied, salesmen are often allocated to one group – say, some types of manufacture, or banking and finance – so they may acquire a deeper knowledge of users' requirements than would otherwise be possible.

Selling computers is a long-drawn-out and complex task. The salesman may first be asked to carry out the initial survey (see the reference to feasibility studies under 'Systems analysis' in Chapter 4) which may take anything from a few weeks to many months, dependent upon the scope and variety of the proposed applications and the activity within the user organisation. The survey is always followed by a comprehensive report which is used as a basis of decision on whether or not to use a computer at all and whether to accept an individual manufaturer's proposal.

When these questions are settled, the user may decide either to purchase or to rent his computer from the manufacturer. In either case, up to two years may elapse before it is actually installed in the user's premises.

During this time, the manufacturer's marketing staff will be in constant contact with the customer. In most cases, they will help him plan his system and give general guidance in mapping out his computer scheme. The salesman, having obtained the contract, will move into the background while a team man, having obtained the contract, will move into the background while a team of technical staff take over, though he will continue to act as the main link betwen manufacturer and user. Since no computer project is without its difficulties, tempers may sometimes get frayed and it may well be the salesman, who knows the customer personnel best, who has to pour oil on troubled water.

Considerable responsibility falls upon the manufacturer's sales staff who will work largely on their own initiative at all levels within the customer organisation. Here they will probably come into contact with all sorts of people from factory and office workers through every grade of manager right to the top.

Once the computer is installed, the salesman generally continues to act as link-man between the user and the manufacturer. In most computer installations, very cordial personal relationships exist between the manufacturer (whose ambassador, so to speak, is the salesman) and the user's management and computer staff.

The computer business is intensly competitive. One of the many reasons for this situation is that, given a certain range of user requirements, there may not be a great deal to choose between one make of computer and another. As a result, it is often the salesman personally most acceptable to the prospective customer who wins the contract. Though good salesmanship and sound technical knowledge are, of course, important, maturity of outlook and absolute integrity weigh at least as much.

Opportunities for successful salesmen in computing are very good. Generally there are excellent prospects for promotion to managerial positions within the manufacturer organisation. There are also many opportunities to move into computer consultancy or into senior positions with computer users if marketing loses its appeal.

Education and Training

The education and training of computer staff is becoming increasingly important and there are many opportunities in these fields. One essential aspect of a manufacturer's support to customers is training and advising their staff. So manufacturers employ lecturers, consultants and specialists in various fields as well as technical authors who prepare reference or educational manuals and other literature.

Lecturers and authors, who may have had experience in computing and have a flair for teaching and writing, are usually graduates. It is quite common for school teachers, for example, to move to a manufacturer to become programming instructors. Manufacturers generally need lecturers and instructors to develop, prepare and conduct courses in all aspects of data processing from key punching to data processing management and appreciation courses for directors and senior managers.

Qualifications generally needed for these teaching and training positions are an acceptable personality, a high standard of education and the ability to express oneself clearly in front of a class as well as in writing, plus skill in imposing discipline. Promotion prospects are good in this growing aspect of the service the supplier provides.

Working with Computer Consultants

Computer consultant firms may be dedicated only to this type of service or be branches of general management consultant organisations. They are employed by prospective or actual computer users to advise them on all or any of the many aspects of computing. Assignments handed to consultants may range from the conducting of the feasibility study through selection of a suitable computer, systems design and programming and the recruitment of outside staff and/or re-training of the user's existing personnel. Consultants may also be called in when a user meets some technical problem that is beyond his regular staff or, for one reason or another, finds his present computer operation unsatisfactory.

An increasing number of consultants are now offering what is known as a 'turnkey' computer operation. This involves sole responsibility from the outset, the consultants finally presenting the client with a ready-made operating computer system, complete with the necessary staff.

As you would expect, most consultants will employ only graduates who have had some practical experience in business or industry and direct acquaintance with the setting up and/or operation of a computer project. Sad to say, very few employ women in jobs involving direct contact with clients (the reason given being that clients would, generally, not have confidence in females!); but most take on suitably qualified women in 'back room' jobs such as programming and the solution of mathematical problems posed by the use of operational research and other scientific management techniques.

A great many consultancy firms now offer a wide variety of training courses. Qualifications for instructors are similar to those required by manufacturers.

Software Houses

Software firms are a special type of consultant whose assignments are generally restricted to programming, the solution of highly technical problems and, perhaps, also systems work. At present computer users (and sometimes manufacturers, too) employ software houses either to tackle problems too tough for solution by their own staff, or because they cannot find suitable staff, or because the job in question is of the once-only variety and would therefore make the employment of full-time specialists uneconomic.

The apparently insatiable demand for skilled and qualified computer staff and the decision of at least one major manufacturer to charge customers separately for hardware and software (implying that they may, if they wish, obtain the latter from other sources) combine to suggest that the number and size of software houses will grow. Since, on the whole, software houses are employed to solve technical rather than human problems, suitably qualified graduate mathematicians and computer scientists may find openings in these establishments directly after leaving university.

The various aspects of consultancy, including software writing, generally appeal particularly to individuals who find satisfaction in problem-solving, who enjoy constant change and are not averse to working, when necessary, for long periods on locations geographically remote from their homes. The larger consultancy firms often have overseas branches and these provide an opportunity for working long or short periods abroad in many different countries.

Other Opportunities

SERVICE BUREAUX

The job of a computer service bureau is to process some or all the aspects of a computer application for customers who either have no computer of their own or whose installations lack the capacity to handle one or more of the tasks they wish to perform. In effect, therefore, they are a rather specialised type of user.

There are many different types of bureau. Some, for example, provide a wide spectrum of services and therefore overlap into the consultant field; others will offer only programming and computer processing; some specialise in data preparation; some are dedicated to fill the needs of only one type of user – for example, stockbrokers or building societies; some expect the user to send his work to them by van or messenger and return results in the same way; others will put remote terminals in a user's premises to give access to the bureau's computer through telephone lines.

In consequence, bureaux offer openings for almost every type of computer job discussed so far in this chapter – including salesmen (who, of course, sell the service, not the computers). Qualifications required by entrants are similar to those needed elsewhere.

FREE-LANCE PROGRAMMING

Some users and consultant firms are prepared to employ programmers who work in their own homes on a part-time basis. Jobs like this are attractive to married women who have worked as programmers before starting a family. Those who accept free-lance work must, however, be prepared to accept the same discipline required in full-time programming and this includes, as a rule, willingness to bring their knowledge up-to-date by taking additional training courses from time to time.

MAKERS OF COMPUTER-RELATED EQUIPMENT

Though almost every manufacturer of computer central processors also makes the entire range of equipment for use with these, there is an increasing number of independent manufacturers who specialise in producing items such as paper tape punches, output printers and various kinds of remote terminal.

Considerable expertise is required to make, sell, service and install these devices, which are generally designed to operate in conjunction with central processors made by all major computer manufacturers. Some types of terminal – notably those that incorporate a TV-type screen – may be supplied with their own self-contained software. And the application of any kind of terminal implies the need for telecommunications knowledge and experience.

Openings therefore exist in these companies for men and women of most skills and experience required by computer manufacturers.

UNIVERSITIES AND COLLEGES

The much publicised shortage of skilled computer staffs has naturally led to rapid expansion in educational facilities. In consequence, there is also a demand for teachers in all kinds of computer subjects in a variety of institutions all over the country.

In conclusion

A Caution for Beginners

We have, in this chapter, tried to give you an indication of the directions in which you may move when you are suitably qualified by education, and if you have the right personal qualities. It is important, though, for you to realise that promotion is not automatic. Not all first jobs provide a good basis or training ground for moving to more ambitious or better-paid work. If, for example, you are a keypunch operator you may not have a chance to become a computer operator; and not everyone who joins as a programmer should hope to become a senior or chief programmer or transfer to systems analysis and design.

Table 3

Jobs and Employers

AREA OF WORK		JOB	COMPUTER USERS	EQUIPMENT SUPPLIERS	CONSULTANTS	SOFTWARE HOUSES	BUREAUX	COLLEGES (ALSO OTHERS)
Operations	→	Data preparation machine operator	*	*			*	
		Ancillary machine operator	*	*			*	
		File librarian	*	*			*	
	→	Computer operator	*	*			*	
	→	Remote terminal operator	*					
	→	Customer engineer		*				
Programming and systems	→	Programmer	*	*		*	*	
		Systems analyst — designer	*	*	*		*	
Overall computer work		DP manager	*	*				
Marketing and sales	→	Sales representative		*		*	*	
Equipment design	→	Design engineer		*				
Software design		Software designer		*		*		
Consulting		Consultant			*	*		
Education and training		Lecturer	*	*	*			*
Non-computer (eg publicity)		Various		*				

→ indicates possible starting jobs

Before taking your first job in computers you should therefore be quite clear about what kind of future openings are available in terms both of your own ability to get a better job (which might depend on your undertaking intensive private study) and of the opportunities provided by your employer. It is fair to say, however, that because the computing world at large is eager to find and use people of real ability, your possession of this coupled with a willingness to work hard should open the way to a future that fully employs your capabilities.

Moving On and Upwards

Table 3 gives a summary of the main opportunities described at some length in the chapter. It also indicates which of these present possible first jobs in the computer field. Studentships and apprenticeships with equipment suppliers have not been included, for simplicity reasons.

A certain amount of mobility is accepted in the computer community, both within and between the different employer sectors. Indeed, the acquisition of wide experience is regarded as important for people who are to be the leaders as the technology and its applications advances. It would be wrong, however, to stress this too strongly, and every new entrant should also bear in mind the need to form ties of loyalty to an organisation which can provide a long-term career with a clear view of what lies beyond employment simply as a computer expert.

A Guide to Salaries in Data Processing

The information given below is taken from a survey carried out in October 1974. Since salaries are constantly changing, and vary for particular areas of the country, you are advised to look at current advertisements for jobs in your area for up-to-date information.

The figures are for the London area. For other major conurbations in England, Scotland and Wales, deduct 10 per cent; for other towns and cities in England, Scotland, Wales and Northern Ireland, deduct 12 per cent *The figures for the middle 50 per cent in each job and grade are given*, to avoid the chance effect of a minority of very low or very high salaries. Actual salary paid will often depend on personal experience and ability.

Data Preparation – Keypunch operators

There is such a wide variation for age and locality that any figures could be misleading. The best people to ask are the officers of the careers service of your Local Education Authority

Computer Operators

Table 4

Junior Operator		Operator		Senior Operator	
£	£	£	£	£	£
1600	2000	1800	2300	2000	2550

Rates for under 21 are generally lower. Many computer operators are required to work shifts. A shift allowance is in some instances part of the basic salary, but in others the shift allowance may be a significant addition to basic salary. The salaries shown are basic and do not include payment for shift working.

Computer Programmers

Table 5

Junior Programmer		Programmer		Senior Programmer	
£	£	£	£	£	£
1850	2300	2300	2950	3000	3650

Programmers may occasionally be asked to work shifts, but overtime, to meet a project deadline, for instance, is a much more frequent feature of this job. Over a year, it could add considerably to the total earnings – but this is something that only the individual employer can advise you on.

The help and guidance of Computer Economics Limited, from whose annual survey of data processing salaries the above figures are adapted, is gratefully acknowledged.

CHAPTER 6

Your Computer Education and Training

A number of organisations are mentioned in this chapter, and a full list of these and their addresses are given in Chapter 7.

In School

Before describing the courses of study designed for people who have already left school, it is important to say that there is beginning to be a good deal of computer education done within secondary schools. A number of enterprising teachers have designed their own courses and the major computer manufacturers have given assistance in these efforts. Computer science is already one subject that can be taken at 'A' level.

General appreciation courses for the 16-18 age group are now available from International Computers Ltd and The National Computing Centre Ltd, and it will not be long before similar studies are done lower down in the school.

As a note to help the teachers we mention here the Computer Education Group. This body provides a focus of information on work in schools, is affiliated to The British Computer Society and publishes a quarterly bulletin 'Computer Education'.

Starting Qualifications

Table 6 provides a summary of the starting jobs available when one has various types and levels of educational qualifications. You will remember that we gave details of the range of such jobs in Chapter 5.

Where can Qualifications in Computing be Obtained?

It should be noted that the starting qualifications set out in Table 6 are not necessarily in computer studies. In the following sections we shall be considering courses of study concerned more directly with computer subjects, and designed particularly for computer specialists.

Table 6

Starting Qualifications

QUALIFICATION NEEDED	STARTING JOB AVAILABLE
Degree. Higher National Diploma, Higher National Certificate (or their equivalent) in relevant subjects	Research, Design and Development Customer Engineering Programming Systems analysis Marketing Education and Training
'A' levels with Mathematics. Ordinary National Certificate or Ordinary National Diploma with Mathematics as main subject	Programming Student Engineering in research, Design, Development or Production Undergraduate Studentship
'A' levels. Ordinary National Certificate or Ordinary National Diploma in Business Studies	Programming Undergraduate Studentship Commercial Studentship Junior Sales
'O' levels with Mathematics	Junior Computer Programming Computer Operating Technician Apprentice
'O' levels	Data Preparation Operating
Good general education	Data Preparation Operating Craft Apprenticeship

We will be concerned, at one end of the scale, with educational courses usually spanning one or more years on a full or substantial part-time basis; and, at the other end, with short training courses of no more than a few weeks (or part-time equivalent) in length. Some of the courses are just as relevant to people who have already started on a career in computing or who began in some other field.

Universities

Full-time courses leading to BSc degrees in Computer Science are available at many universities. Applicants can obtain the full list of courses and make application through the University Central Council for Admissions (UCCA).

These degrees can give exemption from the British Computer Society (BCS) Part I and Part II examinations (to be mentioned later).

Polytechnics and Technical Colleges

The list of places running the various courses described in this section is not necessarily up-to-date and reference should be made to the On Course Bulletin No. 2 'Computer Education in the Technical Colleges' published by the Department of Education and Science. This publication also carries details of the various courses to be described, and of others designed for non-specialists.

For courses in Scotland, reference should be made to the Scottish Education Department.

DEGREES IN COMPUTER SCIENCE

Sandwich courses leading to BSc (CNAA) honours degrees in computing science are available at certain polytechnics. Application for these courses should be made direct to the Admissions Officer.

Again, this list is changing and applicants should refer to the handbook published by the Council for National Academic Awards (CNAA).

All these degree courses have the usual minimum entry qualifications of five GCE subjects including two at 'A' level. In general, the polytechnic courses are integrated with industry by means of periods of industrial experience. The universities generally have one course whereas the polytechnics have a spectrum of courses including honours and ordinary degrees and Higher National Diplomas, which means that students can move up and down according to their abilities.

Some courses, notably at Stafford and Tees-side, do not necessarily require 'A' level mathematics but have been designed to cater not only for students who have studied mathematics or science subjects but also combinations of arts subjects. However, like all degree courses they require good 'O' levels in English or mathematics. All the degree courses in computing science are equally suitable for men or women.

In the polytechnics, students may be college-based or sponsored by an industrial concern which undertakes to provide the necessary industrial training. Some manufacturers and users provide these sponsored students with funds in addition to their grants. The college-based students are placed for their industrial experience by the polytechnic. During these industrial periods each student is expected to make a useful contribution to the work, and undertakes, either individually or in a team, projects which are monitored by the college staff and the industrial tutors.

All honours degree courses are of either three or four years' duration and successful application for such a course ensures that the Local Authority must consider the applicant for a grant but the value of such a grant is dependent upon the applicant's financial circumstances.

Exemptions are possible from the BCS Part I and Part II examinations.

A number of ordinary degree courses qualify for exemption from the Part I examination only.

HIGHER NATIONAL DIPLOMA AND CERTIFICATES

The Diploma course is available under the title of the HND in Computer Studies, and many of these courses give exemption from the British Computer Society Part I examination.

HNDs are available in both polytechnics and technical colleges. They are generally two-year, full-time courses but a small number are of the three year sandwich type.

Generally the entry requirements are four GCE subjects of which one must be at 'A' level or an appropriate Ordinary National Certificate or Diploma. The City & Guilds 747 course (described later) is an alternative entry qualification.

Certain of these Higher National Diplomas in Computer Studies place similar emphasis on both computing and business studies and hence could lead *in due course* to Junior Systems Analyst posts.

The Higher National Diploma in Computer Studies is already available at more that ten polytechnics and colleges. Several polytechnics and some colleges of Technology also offer Higher National Diplomas in Mathematics, Statistics and Computing, and Business Studies with Data Processing. Local Education Authorities have discretionary powers with grants for these courses but most treat applications favourably. In addition some organisations sponsor students on these courses.

For people already in first jobs, an HNC in Computer Studies is already available at a few colleges in England and Wales. In Scotland, an HNC in Data Processing can be taken. These courses run on a part-time basis over a two-year period, with the same entry requirements as the equivalent HND.

BRITISH COMPUTER SOCIETY PART I AND PART II COURSES

As we shall see later, the BCS themselves organise Part I and Part II examinations which, together with computer experience, give full membership to the professional grades of the Society.

The minimum entry for Part I is five GCE 'O' level passes or their equivalent including mathematics and english language. The minimum entry requirement for Part II is the successful completion of Part I, or exemption from it.

Some colleges run courses aimed specifically at the examinations and the duration of the courses offered vary with the college. Some are two or three years part-time, others one year full-time for each part of the examination. Most polytechnics and some colleges of technology offer Part I courses – and ask for some 'A' levels – but Part II is available in a small number of polytechnics. Details of these courses may be obtained from the British Computer Society.

SHORT FULL-TIME (OR EQUIVALENT PART-TIME) COURSES

These courses are available for all types of computer personnel and are more concerned with training for specific jobs than with education in the wider sense.

Programmers

A new qualification designed for trainee or intending programmers has recently been announced by the City & Guilds of London Institute (CGLI), to be called the 746 Basic Certificate in Computer Programming. There are no entry qualifications, and many colleges are expected to offer courses on a full- or part-time basis.

Part-time courses for Junior Programmers already in jobs are also available, leading to the CGLI 747 Certificate in Computer Programming and Information Processing. This provides the study of the basic techniques of programming, coding and operating together with the application of the relevant mathematics and statistics and an introduction to information processing. Entry requirements are usually GCE 'O' level standard or their equivalent. The courses are available generally on a part-time day and evening basis at many technical colleges of further education.

Some manufacturers and users employ Junior Programmers at the age of eighteen. It is normal for these employees to have gained two GCE 'A' levels and they are often required to attend some of the part-time courses mentioned above or courses provided by the manufacturers themselves.

Operators

Another area of computer education which overlaps somewhat with the CGLI 747 course is that of Computer Operators. The title of Computer Operator should not be confused with that of Machine Operator. Applicants for Computer Operator posts generally require some programming knowledge and have four GCE 'O' level subjects but some employers prefer them to have some 'A' levels. They are normally given a four-week introductory course by the manufacturers and then complete their training on site in six to nine months. Applicants for posts of Computer Operators should be warned that they are likely to have to work on shifts.

In addition to the 747 course, the course for the Royal Society of Arts (RSA) Computer Operators Certificate varies according to the various technical colleges and colleges of commmerce which run the course. It is designed to test the knowledge of those involved in day-to-day operating of computer installations comprising central processor, data file equipment, input and output devices whether in a commercial, administrative or scientific environment. The duration of the course varies according to the college but is usually a one-year day release course.

In Scotland, an equivalent Operators Certificate is available under the auspices of the Scottish Business Education Council (SCOTBEC).

Systems Analysts

Vacancies for systems analysts are usually filled either by program-mers with some years of programming and commercial experience behind them, or by people with a business background who are taught the necessary computer techniques. There is a growing trend, however, to recruit graduates specially for systems work and put them through comprehensive business, computer and systems training.

The National Computing Centre (NCC) Basic Course in Systems Analysis is operating in many polytechnics and technical colleges, either on a full-time six-week or part time basis. It is recommended that entrants to the course should have had *either* at least six month's data processing experience in some relevant capacity, together with the successful completion of a suitable business course *or* at least one year's experience in a business environment, together with the successful completion of a preliminary course of study in data processing. A certificate is awarded by NCC to successful candidates.

There is also an NCC Higher Certificate in Systems Analysis, which can be taken by anyone who *either* holds the NCC Basic Certificate in Systems Analysis *and* has subsequently been employed primarily as a systems analyst for not less than 12 months *or* has obtained admission by passing a qualifying examination. (This option will be available until June 1977.)

A longer (six-month) Diploma course is available in Scotland only, under the auspices of SCOTBEC. It is designed for post-degree or post-experience students, and gives exemption from the BCS Part I examination.

The Private 'Sector'

Some of the 'short' courses described, notably the CGLI 746 and the NCC Basic Systems Certificate, are (or will be) run by private business organisations either for their own staff or for the general public.

Also, it has already been said that the equipment suppliers and others run a variety of short courses designed for their customers and clients.

UK Co-ordinating Committee for Examinations in Computer Studies (UKCC)

The qualifications described and awarded by the CGLI, RSA, NCC and SCOTBEC have the approval of the committee, and awards are made jointly with this body.

Computing as a Profession

The British Computer Society has already been mentioned in the context of exemptions from its examinations and college courses which prepare candidates for the examinations.

The Part I examination leads to the grade of Associateship, and the Part II examination to the grade of Membership after five years of appropriate experience. The senior grade of Fellowship can be awarded after a further period of three years' relevant work in computing.

The Society provides the main focus of professional competence in computing, and has a total membership of over 22,000.

Two other bodies, the Data Processing Managers Association and the
Institute of Data Processing, are concerned with the particular needs
of DP managers and practitioners in computer application respectively. Some colleges run courses leading to the qualifications of the
Institute which is particularly concerned with the application of
computers in accounting and administration.

CHAPTER 7

Where to get more Information

General

A list of useful publications and addresses is given below. All the publications should be available either from the teachers responsible for careers advice in schools or from the careers service of your local Education Authority.

The 'Computer Courses' series published by the National Computing Centre covers all courses in the United Kingdom. A useful general publication is the Educational Yearbook published by the British Computer Society.

Work at School

For general advice, reference can be made to:

> The Computer Education Group,
> North Staffordshire Polytechnic,
> Computer Centre,
> Blackheath Lane,
> Stafford.

University Courses

Information can be obtained either direct from particular universities or by reference to the list published by:

> The University Central Council for Admissions,
> G.P.O. Box 28,
> Cheltenham,
> Gloucestershire.

Courses in Polytechnics and Technical Colleges

Information can be obtained either direct from particular colleges or by reference to the On Course Bulletin No. 2 'Computer Education' published by:

> The Department of Education & Science,
> (Further Education Information Officer),
> 39 York House,
> London, SE1 7PH

For courses in Scotland, reference should be made to colleges, or at:

> The Scottish Education Department,
> St. Andrews House,
> Edinburgh 1.

If more detail is required on particular courses, the following bodies can be referred to, as appropriate:

> Council for National Academic Awards,
> 3 Devonshire Street,
> London, W1.

> The British Computer Society,
> 29 Portland Place,
> London, W1.

> City and Guilds of London Institute,
> 76 Portland Place,
> London, W1.

> Royal Society of Arts,
> 6-8 Adam Street,
> Adelphi,
> London, W.C.2.

> The National Computing Centre Limited,
> Oxford Road,
> Manchester M1 7ED

> Scottish Business Education Council,
> 22 Gt. King Street,
> Edinburgh 3.

> Scottish Technical Education Council,
> 38 Queen Street,
> Glasgow, C.1.

'Private Sector' Courses

Details of these are to be found in the Press, but in general it will be found that employers have full information held by their training officers or by the manager responsible for computer activities.

Professional Status

For information on the question of gaining a professional qualification, you should write to The British Computer Society.

Employers

For opportunities with computer users and others, you should consult your local Careers Office or careers teacher, and keep an eye on the local and national Press.

If you are thinking of a post with a major computing equipment supplier, you should write to the Personnel Department. Some useful addresses are as follows:

Burroughs Machines Ltd.,
Heathrow House,
Bath Road,
Cranford,
Hounslow,
Middlesex.

Control Data Ltd.,
22a St. James Square,
London, S.W.1.

Honeywell Information Systems Ltd.,
Gt. West Road,
Brentford,
Middlesex.

IBM (United Kingdom) Ltd.,
101 Wigmore Street,
London, W.1.

International Computers Ltd.,
ICL House,
Putney High Street,
London, S.W.15.

The National Cash Register Co. Ltd.,
206-216 Marylebone Road,
London, N.W.1.

Univac Division of Sperry Rand Ltd.,
65 High Holborn Viaduct,
London, S.W.1.